THE LITTLE GOD OF DAMAGE LIMITATION

Aileen La Tourette

First Published in 2021
By Live Canon Poetry Ltd
www.livecanon.co.uk

978-1-909703-58-2

A CIP catalogue record for this book is available from the British Library.

THE LITTLE GOD OF DAMAGE LIMITATION

Aileen La Tourette is and will always be the proud mother of Nicholas Joshua and Reuben Luke. She has published two volumes of poetry with Headland, *Downward Mobility* and *Touching Base*. The oldest of *Poetry Review's* 'New Poets' in 1992, her poems have appeared in a number of Live Canon anthologies in recent years, in *The Forward Book of Poetry 2014*, and in 2016 her poem 'the Diving Horse' won First Prize in the Live Canon International Competition. She has had a number of radio plays broadcast on Radio 4, most of them directed by Jane Morgan, one by Ned Chaillet. She retired from lecturing in Creative Writing at Liverpool John Moores University in 2011, and completed a qualification in poetry therapy in 2015. She facilitates a poetry group at Mind in Birkenhead, which has kept going online during the past two years.

Acknowledgements

Thank you first always to Nick, Reuben's brother, my older son, best reader of these poems, for his help and support and being my main, best and sometimes only reason for carrying on. Thanks also to David, Reuben's father, my husband, to my dear Bubble-friend and long-term support, poet Gladys Mary Coles whose early comments helped shape these poems, to my brother Bill for his interest in them and for the way he has been here and supported us from across the Atlantic, my aunt Adele Blong for her visits and emails, cousin Monica Wagner for listening, my sisters Amelie and Adele, my brother Thomas, my onetime college roommate Lynn Langford. Thanks to Jenny Newman for her friendship and generous response to this work, to Jill Teague, my Poetry Therapy mentor who was with me when the sequence began, to Rabbi Janet Burden, who has stayed close, and to friends Michael Wherly, Vera Lustig, Tricia Hagan and Gillian Homeri, for their presence during these hard years. Thanks to Cate Jacobs and John Feeney for their differing modes of moral and spiritual support. I would also like to thank poet Denise Riley and novelist David Grossman for their generous work that meets me in another way.

Contents

Minding the Gap	7
The Bridge	9
Dear Garbage Truck,	10
Dear Gun I Have Never Wanted Until Now,	11
Dear George Washington Bridge,	13
To Any Passing Bridge:	15
Dear Merseyrail Train	16
Dear Rush Hour,	17
Dear Blade, Knife or Razor,	18
River Again	19
Dear Tree,	20
Dear Spontaneous Combustion,	21
Dear Snow Globe,	23
Dear Sneese,	25
On Methodology	26
The Mother Runners	27
Dear Boredom,	29
Dear Broken Heart,	30
Dear Ceiling Fan,	31
Dear Pockets,	32
Dear Sword,	34
Radio You	35
Too Cold to Snow	36
Dear Exfoliation Gel,	38
Mudpie Mother	39
Dear Poison,	40
Dear Window,	41
The Little God of Damage Limitation	42
Dear Window Again	44
Tapers	45
Ibiza	47
Gobsmacked	49
Be Still	50

For Reuben

Minding the Gap

That moment in Eden
when the apple eats
you and eats you

when everything twists
like the bridge opening
to let the boat through

the open-backed stairs
to the cellar or anywhere,
the space that glares -

they name it here, blare
a warning: *Mind the Gap-*
I like that about England,

one of the many things
I wish I'd told you.

Maybe you'd say *yeah*
it was the same the time

the kitchen ceiling fell
around me in my high chair,

already a bit risky, that
height. That moment in Eden

when the apple eats you
and you know the secret

of the divided bridge,
the raining ceiling,

even if they miss you,
this time.

Now I mind the gap
like the flock
of pigeons crooning

on their slab
in the brutalist station,
like your red carrycot.

The Bridge

is not a bridge. It's a concrete platform
overlooking the East River, which is a strait.
Nothing is as it seems. A concrete platform,
concrete stick figure on it thinking no one
she knows would have to see, if she. *True,*
her late son agrees. *But think of my brother.*
You're not Ophelia, Mother. Let alone – to be
or not to be is not your scene. Halfway houses
are more up your street, yes? She turns around,
her two black patent shoes like papooses – *Papice?*
he offers gleefully – holding the swaddled babies
of her feet. *More like the polished shoes of two*
NYPD cops who've seen it all before, guiding
a slightly crazy old lady across the street when
the light turns green. Babies or cops, they do.

9

Dear Garbage Truck,

You grind away at the bottom of the alley, digesting slime,
slop, scrapings from plates, mashed crap, gristle, stuff
still wrapped in cellophane past Use By dates. I think of
mad saints, what you chew to mucilage their grace,
penance, craziness: Thérèse of Lisieux heaping her plate with what
the other nuns left in that ravenous place. Margaret Mary Alacoque
licking up spews and leakages for Jesus. I keep failing to go that mad,
a kind of failure not much addressed. Dervish in the dervish dawn,

I could join gloved men dancing bins onto your ramp, tipping them
into your chute. I could sling stout green torsos around, manhandle them
back to the curb. Grief has made me strong in all the wrong ways.
You low from streets away as empty tampax tubes roll on the concrete.
Your peristalsis gas hangs in the air as Teresa of Avila comes in
on that old radio: *I would grind myself to powder to fulfil your holy will.*

You'd never take me on, so take me in. I can't do music any more
except your drone, Rag and Bone's Gregorian of loss to hoof-clops
in the grey afternoon. I'd take the leap of waste, pulp, mulch to roughage,
landfill. Let me land fill. Bodies in movies dangle over dumps from forklifts.
Widows jump like Dido, or get thrown. More fitting, this filth-suttee, for me,

a mother here after her child is gone. A face swims up on concrete
as your growl fades, maybe wondering if piecemeal is the only peace –
or tangled in rubbish-music like seaweed, heart-freezing as tunes in shops
but tines, not strings, sharpened on pumice in the throat – waiting till it goes away,
the seizure, the tremor from nowhere, the bends,
the sudden rapture of so many edges,
such small ends.

Dear Gun I Have Never Wanted Until Now,

In cop shows you play a kind of
metal hand grafted on, locked to
the fingers at arm's length, straight
arm pointing without a quiver -

maybe that's what you become
for everyone who holds you
all the time, finger in the circle
of the trigger like a wedding ring

- the bracelet of a steering wheel
seems much the same for people
whose wrists know its angles.
I never wore that bangle either,

never felt that kind of confidence,
believed it could be second nature.
Probably a mistake. I can cut bread,
meat, chop veg without going off-piste,

used to hold the glass rod under
my tongue without crunching it,
sucking in the blur of Mercury.
I know the itch of risk is universal,

but we scratch it differently. My son
showed me the glass bus shelter where
he'd met the dealer, something gone
forever. Over. Then he was, over

night. Over my head. Misadventure at
home. Nightmare closer than daylight
can ever come. His heart, a combination
he thought was just right. No way to know.

I pass the bus stop wishing for a capsule
of cyanide to chew, a lightning bolt, you.
He never fired you either though he did
karate chops and punches, wrists straight,

concentration on his face – Hemingway's
rifle feels more righteous than a cold Colt
Something. My son was a writer. But I'm no
Annie Oakley. Where would I even get you?

I don't get you. But if you were here, if
you were in the house, you'd call the tune
we've all heard in a million films. Always
the same. People lift you as I write, like

lifting a glass. *Cheers*. He liked that show.
Your health. What a joke. *L'chaim*, we said,
my Jewish son and I. *To life* sticks in my throat.
I can't go there. But you I will not toast.

Dear George Washington Bridge,

Your knife hides
the incision it
makes in space,
a grey blade
hung suspended
like indecision
when it's too late
to change, two states
already joined, land
water and sky already
left behind. We don't
all jump at the same
time or jump at the
same things. The Dutch
hated the Palisades,
saw demons smoking
up in your dark lining
of sharp rock. My son
was often homesick
for a Holland I never
drained for him, only
a narrow stretch
like your shadowy
Hudson Valley,
Irving's Sleepy Hollow
ringing with the Headless
Horseman's hoofbeats,
Rip van Winkle's snores
for two decades. He shakes
his head at me, shaking
these stale mythologies
for traces, stalking him
through fiction, history:
Layfayette re-crossing
the Atlantic, coming back
to see the valley in peace,
comfortably old now,
caped like he used to be,

Robin to his brother's
Batman, tall, broader
than de Gaulle – why
am I stalling, killing
time instead of falling?
Where is that peace Jonathan
Edwards seems to locate in
'... *a solitary place on the banks
of Hudson's River for secret
converse with God*'? Secrecy,
sacred and profane. We'd talk
about that. Barrel cables swing
like cradles, *Rockabye baby*
- no way in. Hell smells
like a giant ice tray. Freeze me
on your walkway. I'd dive less
swan than cannonball, becoming
someone else's story like the one
where the cop stops a suicide
by threatening to shoot. True.
He stares sternly, this man-child
I failed. *So, it's all about you?*

To Any Passing Bridge:

You all have the same idea,
advertised in a steel hieroglyph
internationally recognized, most
successful over the Yangtze, next
the Golden Gate, though they're
braiding gold mesh for a matching
net. Prince Edward Viaduct, Toronto,
a magnet for suicide until they wove
a *luminous veil.* Some people think
it's wrong to catch people when
they fall. Keep the lines clean, don't
bandage bridges, *besides, if they're
gonna do it, they're gonna do it,
right? They'll find another bridge?*
Funny thing is, no. They don't. Once
a famous bridge becomes impossible
to jump from, almost nobody chooses
an unknown one. They go home.
They hang in. Did you just shrug?
Are you beside me on this invisible
bridge I am not going to jump from
into the family tree of ghosts between
the river and the sky? I feel your big
hand, basketry of fingers red and raw
in the cold wind, catch mine and squeeze.

Dear Merseyrail Train,

You only have three cars
instead of the long trains
that bang in and out of
New York stations,
graffiti-daubed. Still
three is mystical,
I believe you're good
at clarifying the mind-
body split without
a lot of abstract chat?
Do I mean soul
and body? Do I mean
amplifying it? Believe
me, I don't know. How
many of us on this
platform ask how
fast, how painful,
would it be, as we
wait, told we are
delayed by *a person
under a train?* Sat
finally in the train,
but not finally –
sat in the irony
of being *late*,
the nerve-jingle
of the silly little bell
that rings, twice.

Dear Rush Hour,

My son's rush hour came just
after midnight or thereabouts,
what traffic in his brain, what
bottlenecks, what pile-ups,
impossible to know. Impossible
the bated breath. The legs under
the desk, the driver's seat he never
left. Keyboards for fingers, deft
no more. Impossible the brake,
the heart's accelerator guessed,
impossible the road ahead,
the stupid metaphor. The missed
turns, blind spots, soundless crash,
tailspin, veer, black ice, a cliff.
The stupid metaphors that strain.
The driver's seat he never left again.

Dear Blade, Knife or Razor,

You hurt. I know that.
As a kid I once drew
a blade across my wrist,
another when too old
for that exhibitionist
nonsense. Stitches,
stitches, we all get
stitched up. Next
time would be It.
But someone would
get stuck with the mess,
somebody have that
picture in her head
again and again and again
like acid reflux. I couldn't
even pick my victim,
let alone be them.

River Again

you flow fast up here
the current sidewinds in
catches people
flowers on the railings signal
shrines to our failings
and why not celebrate
what sinks instead of swims?
Given it's a given.
My lost saints give way
to these ersatz bouquets
gratefully. Why wait
for heaven when
there's this signpost,
this stop sign,
ribbon?

Dear Tree,

Think of me as laundry.
Only your spot between
graveyard and library, not
too near the playground,
feels appropriate, kind of
off in a corner, private.
This is not a cowboy movie,
no sheriff, no paparazzi,
strictly low-key. Don't
take it personally. I can't
stick life without
my child. QED.
You seem to shake
in sympathy or palsy.
Anxiety? You writhe
in the wind, gasp
for breath, hyperventilate
into the sky. It's not
about me. You fuss,
obsessing over layers,
what to keep on, what
to take off, always wrong,
bark goosefleshed –
scarred with self-harm?
Leaves hurled,
nicotine-saturated,
brittle under my shoes,
eau de nostalgie
heavy on the wind,
to cover the bulimic
reek? Earlier this afternoon,
you were hallucinating June.
Every year you have
a breakdown on cue.
Funny asking you to loan
me a low bough, you have so
many hang-ups of your own.

Dear Spontaneous Combustion,

You are *the death by fire*
originating without
an apparent external
source of ignition,
a phenomenon that
attracted the attention
not only of the medical
profession but of the laity
in the mid-nineteenth century.
Cases of SC had ten things
in common, including:
alcoholism; being elderly
and female; hands and feet
falling off; the fire not
hurting anything else,
even things it touched,
but leaving *a residue*
of greasy, fetid ashes,
very offensive in odour.
Ok, it definitely seems to me
I qualify. Although my feet
and hands are still attached,
they're always up for grabs,
fingertips tapping away, taking
dictation, secretive, resentful
as secretaries, toes still mad
at those old stupid shoes,
fed up with the workload. No
fireworks, I'd go quietly,
primed with wine. I do not
think I'm Joan of Arc even
in my cups, nor have I ever
aspired to high witchcraft, or
martyrdom – well not since
my Rose of Lima days at ten,
pulling my belt tight, hooking
the crucifix. This is not political.

I don't even have to hold my nose
for the offensive odour I won't smell.
Someone else with have to dispose
of the greasy, fetid ash. Oh, well.
– So if you need someone
to practice on, like an apprentice
in a hair salon? I'm on.

Dear Snow Globe,

I used to think you
were a kind of heaven,
so protected. I think my
son did too. We both shook
down your snow, wanted to go
inside the bubble to lie
under whiteness, tasting
it like manna, hungry
tongues slowly growing
numb. He slipped and slid
beneath cold layers where
I try to follow, knocking
on the glass, wanting to smash
my way in. I try not to panic,
think I might shrink in the cold sea,
maybe shrink in heat. I am shrinking,
slowly. It's taking a long time to grow
down to snow globe size. His brother
and his father call to me. He waves
me away, his blue lips framing syllables,
*I fell. You stay. I stumbled. You hobble
on.* My lips frame *No way* but thumbelina
through the long tall days. Sometimes
the little dog pulls me like an empty sleigh.
Sometimes he's with me. I shake your ovals,
your crystal domes, your plastic eggs, looking
for him. He liked your closed pods, I know.
Like I do. I can't break them. I can't go home.

2.

little heads on pedestals,
snow globes. You loved
them with the tolerance
we give each other's
harmless follies. Kissed
with blasphemy, the ones
with creepy, stigmatized
saints. No blood falls on
the snow. Little heads,
their landscaped thoughts
on show. They line the dining
room windowsill, as you know.

Dear Sneeze,

Victorian women pop off from chills, quite often,
they're always 'catching a chill' like a bus to heaven
or hell. It seems to come upon them fast from standing
in the rain for a minute or two and then it's touch and go.

I walk the dog in all weathers and nothing happens. I am
often underdressed, underestimate the wind chill factor
without even trying but it gets me nowhere fast. I seem to thrive
on all this exercise and braving the West Wind which isn't Shelley's

breath of autumn's beauty just a blast of air slamming my face,
quite welcome really. Then again I guess death by sneezing
has a farcical allure. You could sneeze yourself senseless?
Your heart skips a beat when you sneeze so if you kept on skipping them,

you'd peg out ? People could make those roses out of Kleenex
and bobby pins with red nail polish stroked on them I learned
how to make from a friend called Allenah Lorenz when
I had an infected quick from biting my nails. I really liked

that afternoon, it might have been the high spot of my life,
lying in bed making tissue roses with Allenah Lorenz, dotting
them with red nail polish. I think I'll leave that as a last request,
that everyone make Kleenex roses with bobby pins and spot them

red because I've gone off in a clot of snot. The pepperpot scene from Alice
in Wonderland can be read at the funeral. Everyone to blow their noses
all together please. Better than hiccups which killed that old fascist
Pius XII, whose yellowing wax effigy at the back of St. Patrick's

was melted down for votive candles when it started slip into disrepair
and make him look like someone he'd refuse to sit near. I don't wish
to imitate his Unholiness in any way– my son was proud of me when
I refused to set foot in the Vatican. So just sneeze my head off please.

On Methodology

People get details from Exit,
a serious Australian organization,
or go to Dignitas in Switzerland
which costs them. On the whole,
I'd go the Exit route. Swiss women
voted against the vote, which never
made sense. It does dispense death
painlessly, if coldly. For a fee. Exit
gives you recipes, even machinery.
Thomas Merton died from a fire
in the bath, something more elementary.
Fire and water meet, electricity strikes
the flesh. Not such a bad role model,
old Merton, if a bit old hat, a monk
to boot – my son would not approve.
Too Catholic, if maverick. *Besides,*
he'd argue, *his death was an accident.*
The poor bastard just wanted heat,
(like me with drugs) he wouldn't add.
I see them fussing like men can, arranging
the electric fire on a shelf over the tub,
carefully calculating the right dose.
At least Merton was old, I might
say. He'd agree. *Yes, and my brother*
would be, overnight. You're no Roman,
Mother. No, I'd have to agree. *I only hope*
you basked, before the white mass of avalanche.

The Mother Runners

It came so easily to you –
drugs/heart/some combination
of the two. We'll never know.
Fast, quiet, now I wait for it to hit
and it stays back. I walk the dog,
get fit. Drop weight. What is this
shadow life I live? – shadows don't
exactly live. I slither on the surface
of the world, swim into another week
feeling posthumous astonishment -
another night gone by without
taking me with it. Why? is not even
a question, though it is. Sheer blind
stupid life goes on as they say only
much stupider than anyone knows
unless they unlive here like the woman
who stopped by yesterday from
Compassionate Friends, all frenzied
activity after six years – nods, smiles, tics
I recognize. We're all tics, we mothers
in this horror club. We're all activity.
She does charity runs, organizes them.
I can see the point of running, running,
we all run, chasing our dead sons,
running from their ends,
running from the present to redo a past
we can't. Louise Bourgeois' huge sculptures
in the Turbine Hall of the Tate Modern
back in that other life where there were
art galleries and television, civilization
I suppose, – *I Do/I Undo/I Redo*
– climbing up her mirrored towers in those
old Rapunzel days. She was a good witch,
once upon a time. Yes. I'm babbling,
you'd say that. Just like you did when
you were a kid, babbling away, later

we'd talk about the Tower of Babel
all that good Biblical stuff that failed
to save you somehow now I'm
with the mothers running into walls
hoping to stun ourselves stupid
and numb. Running till we fall.

Dear Boredom,

I can't die of you now.
I could when life was good.
It's not an option when
every day is this whiteout,
this howl. This keen.
When I'm a banshee.
I remember your deaths.
They were pleasant,
in the way bad things
were all quite wonderful
while life was whole.

I was a person then.
My son was alive.
I got bored, even with him
on his high horse, before
it ran away with him.
I never get bored any more.
I don't think people who say
they're dying of boredom
have a clue what holidays
they're on, what spa weekends
they've won. They should die
of boredom all they can,
while they have time.

Dear Broken Heart,

Pure knuckle punching
way above your weight,
you break every day,
knit up at night in secret
like Penelope's tapestries,
your own alibi for not dying,
going at your own speed,
beating your own drum,
welterweight throwing
every fight but going
back into the ring,
why do they think
it's livers that regenerate
so they can re-break?

Dear Ceiling Fan,

Death by fandango might be hard to arrange
but on the other hand your blades spin fast.
If I could find a ladder, climb climb climb
– it's a high ceiling - stick my head
in your chopped-up chopper blades
you might just chop it off and helicopt my life
to its demise, lobbing it and my trunk together
but separate forever onto the bed below, though
this being my cousin's apartment which she's spent
a fortune renovating it would not be kind or nice
– those words she lives up to and I revile in my ill
soul where they have no place. Still, I'd hate her to find
me like John the Baptist on his platter or the horsehead
in *The Godfather* in her sofa bed, a pool of blood around
me and a spatter everywhere on her new paintwork,
her gleaming stripped-down floor, her rug, her furniture,
my eyes all starey, flies squeezed through the screen by
the time she gets home wanting to sit down and drink
a glass of wine. She'd never forget it and might lose
her very good mind which is trying to save the planet,
at least some of it. I guess death by fandango here in
her apartment isn't on the cards, maybe somewhere else
a fan churns like the chopper blades in *Mash* while
they sing *Suicide is painless/ it brings on many changes/
and I can take or leave it if I may.* I'll stash your blades
away, a notion for later. Apocalypse not now. Maybe in
a neutral space – a tropical hotel? Has anyone ever used
you as an ersatz guillotine? You shred the air, every breath
sliced like vegetables, words juiced like fruit, rotate
like mechanical days, hypnotize people to make them stay.

Dear Pockets,

I've always loved you, two
by two on tunics and loose
smocky things, jackets, coats,
places for hands to go, those
hands I flash on hacking off
since they stroked his cool cheek.
No one should ever know what
they have known. Lady Macbeth
hands, meeting the first touch
of him head-on, and the last,
neither of us ever thinking it was.
Casual enough good night, *We
will make the best of it* – meaning
this time, his taper going on –
We will, his reply. Touch, kiss
on the forehead nerve endings
remember like piano fingers,
play and replay. Pockets. Virginia
used you to make certain not to
fail again. You come in handy,
hold tissues, mostly, but good
to know you could drown me
like a litter of kittens, no problem.

My hands fall into you like graves
anyway, places of rest, nests, shred
wet tissues like mice, barnacle
small rocks I put there like talismen
- or scouts, looking to heavier stones
ahead? I have another son. Please
pocket these sad hands as best
you can, for him, run the knuckles
aground on your false bottom when
they bottom out. *I shall lay hands
on myself* says Tolstoy's heroine.
They tap these words, my alien hands.

They fatten you. They chop and cook,
hold phones, lift cups and glasses,
lots. *Pockets full of posy* protected
against the pox. Small pockets drop
like parachutes into the day's grey
freefall. Night has deep pockets, amen.

Dear Sword,

Do you just stand there and wait
while I fall over, sideways or straight?

– so you're the fall guy in our duo?
– but we both need to be on our toes,
get our timing absolutely right –

it always sounds so easy, *falling
on your sword*. But I'm not privy
to the choreography. How do you get
the angle right, first time? Otherwise,

a human pincushion? Mishima fished
his guts for nobleness and found his,
I guess. But he was nuts. I can't seem
to go totally Mishima. It may come.

We went completely Murakami
in the Lewisham Library. I read
the latest one aloud in his room,
not sure he would approve.

Titles gleam from the shelves
next door, letters sinking in
like tiny light bulbs made
to jab and twist like bayonets.

Radio You

I tune you in when
I can find you
- when I can bear to
twirl the dials in my head
till your voice arrives

just itself
nothing and
no one else

sometimes
sometimes
sometimes

I let myself believe
you broadcast live

Too Cold to Snow

The stillness in the waiting room – no windows,
only light from the door we came in from and will go
out through, to which our eyes return as we fret
in our classroom chairs, three rows facing each other,
lots of empty seats. Only a few people here, as there were

when I came here with you so long ago and yesterday,
hoping the doctor could do what it took, then down
the road to take an overdose of books from the library,
hoping some Holy Ghost would flap out of those covers –
we both thought it could happen, why not then when

we needed it so much? The stillness comes down from
the ceiling, rises from beneath the floorboards, subdues
everyone, reduced to words made flesh in the hush,
doughballs overflowing our seats even if we don't, an ooze
of souls – you'd grimace, shrug down into your book,

a grown man struggling with Valium, hating the dusk
it settles over you, finding a little smoke of heroin can cut
right through - *weak as your secrets,* says our friend in AA.
I've come to hear about the you the doctor knew, ask him
things he cannot answer. The stillness feels stalled, like when

we used to say it was *too cold to snow.* I don't know what
we meant exactly, it snows in the Poles, and we were in
New Jersey, as you know. We had to find some reason
for the vague sky hanging at an angle, the hazy purple glow
at the horizon, the trees gone quiet, almost like labour

slowing down just when you want to get it over with -
you know, the God of the Cathars contracted to make
room for everything. I always liked that act of generosity
the Catholics made them burn for, calling their churches
Synagogues of Satan. We could talk about that, my lapse

from what the Cathars called the *Church of Wolves,*
your Liberal Judaism, staunch and sacred. If I made
a crass joke about God panting away like a dog
in labour, you'd shake your wonderfully shaped head
and roll your dark, incisive eyes, hooded and wise,

much of the time you were here, even in childhood.
Much of the time. You'd nod. You liked talking
about God. Words were your drug of choice, much
of the time. Much of. The time. We'd sit here, take
on us the mysteries – I hear you sigh *You're not Lear,*

for G-d's sake, nor I - , not saying either name. But
focused, your open face showing. The shadows
wouldn't roll up neatly but they wouldn't be like this.
The sky I can't locate behind the low ceiling would
melt manna-moments on our tongues, kids tasting snow.

Dear Exfoliation Gel,

Genies in bottles don't come cheap,
but you weren't so expensive either,
brought by the Avon Lady down
the lane to rub away a layer of me

in sooty little rolls of dirt, sweat,
skin. Vanishing cream is an old
name. Vaseline. Lemon cold
cream made velvet in the glass

like a Venetian mask, one summer,
long ago. It must be the rubbing
that matters, like sanding floors,
like cleaning the nuns' medals

at the shore like we used to do,
even longer ago, rubbing them
with dry sand. Now I need you.
Exfoliate me down to ground zero,

I'll rub as long as it takes till
I'm smoke. Fizz me into white
rime, merengue me into goo.
Leave a rim around the tub

if you must. I am a rim now,
without him, my missing son
who will not return, though
the rim I perch on is a hopeless

hope. No need for fiery chariots.
No Elijahs. Just exfoliate me
like a tree. Quietly. No hysteria.
I hear trees sigh outside, resigned

but wistful at the slow rate
of exfoliation. Every year a leaf
or so less twists off. It takes
decades. We say they celebrate.

Mudpie Mother

Mudpacks in the bathroom,
minerals from the Dead Sea
where no one swims. We drifted
in that grease-bay, you and I,
given a seat, you on my lap,
afterwards, in the sweaty bus
by the Israelis, generous,
impossible. You shaped me
as you sat. You slapped my dough,
the kiln of your mouth baked
my words. Now I am scarecrow,
effigy, ancient and implacable,
Rachel bleeding out into the world
red blood-ribbons in a pantomime,
pulled back in, bled again. But liquid.
Corpuscled. Real, pouring blood.
Walking the dog, going where I do,
Catching those eyepatch-glimpses of you.
Here a hairline, there a dark eye. A stance,
a gait. A trace. I bitch along snuffling for
those truffles, mud-pie mother still shaped
in the mould of your hands. Day will come
when I need Springsteen, Dylan, Thea Gilmore,
all your music I flee now. Leave cafes,
boutiques. Leonard, Alison Krauss.
Plant. Jesus, make me deaf. Blind,
dumb, stupid, gone. Work miracles
backwards in my case. This mud banshees
wails keens hums howls. All day long.
Now I understand how saints did crazy
things for Jesus, unable to bear his ancient
suffering and death. Eating the unspeakable.
Hair shirts and hunger. It was the dark mother
in those virgins, punctured women
leaking air like tyres, letting it all out,
flattening themselves, it was this mother
made of mud who would become nothing
again and again, wandering in the ruins
chanting and humming, this bag lady
dozing in the bones, sucking the marrow.

Dear Poison,

So many household poisons live under the sink.
Kurt Vonnegut's mother went that way but
in time for him to live. Now it's too late to die
before my child and I'm already posthumous,

but take you in with calculating eyes,
cleansers and toilet ducks, mouse and rat poison
I buy remembering his phobia, because
he thought there were rats in the old house –

I thought they were mice but watched
like a cat while he was here. Got rid quick.
Now I envy them their little blue pellets,
regret his leftover prescriptions my brother

took back to the surgery in the second year
when the fog began to lift, layers pull away
like bandages, like mummy cloths unwinding
so slowly, unbelief going, never completely –

I don't think he ever believed, or guessed.
He went in a cloud of unknowing. *if there's
such a thing as a pleasant death,* the doctor said.
 I wanted life's unpleasantness for him, along

with all the rest. Not this. Not this. Not this.
Everyone keeps half an eye on poison, picks
a little bit, drugs, debt, everyone tries for
a homeopathic dose like he did, hoping

for the best, to wake up again, rueful,
bittersweet: another comeback. Not him,
though I go on hoping hopelessly, because
I have no choice. Hope's spring is the kind

that whacks you in the face, Jack-in-the-Box
that pops up when you turn the key in the front
door, when you leave the book open in his room,
when you breathe, sip wine like blood-red seas.

Dear Window,

Poking the pistachio shells for leftovers,
my fingernails are scimitars hooking

the nutmeat's tiny green and purple filet.
The pistachio safari soothes my hands,

better than hand cream I don't use.
It's hunt and gather on a small scale,

something primitive and savage to do
in a very minor key, not like the windows

I imagine bursting through, not this one
in the dining room, it's too low down,

though I could throw something right
through the middle of it, shatter, smash,

crash, only I'd have to clear the mess
up and cut myself in silly minor ways

and feel worse, failing at everything.
This mood is not worthy of you.

There is a window upstairs that might do
but I am sitting here picking pistachios

out of their shells and thinking of you
how you believed in the *Shekinah*,

indwelling Presence waiting for release
by us. How much *Shekinah* you released.

The Little God of Damage Limitation

Make veg soup on a rainy Monday a.m. Paraphrase rainy
old Ecclesiastes as he always should be paraphrased, i.e.:
The generations of women are like onions, tomatoes, beans,
sieved into soup you wouldn't eat though the making
is for you somehow, like everything. Your absence goes on

raining in the kitchen right into the pot with onions, cabbage,
carrots. You'd like the croutons, baguette cubes in garlic
and olive oil. The spitting on the hob would make you frown
and turn the gas down. *Have you turned the oven on,* you'd
ask, exasperated when I forgot that vital first step. I still

forget, still make boeuf bourguignon sometimes, as if the scent
could smoke you right out of your room, or the ground. *This is a one-
person kitchen,* you'd insist, and only you could put the food away
after we shopped - one place you'd go, down to Morrisons.
I skate up and down your favourite aisle on thin ice, waiting

to lie there in the lino, kick and scream like a deprived child.
Later I find poems for my group, good ones I can't discuss
with you, even over the phone, even hearing boredom in your voice.
The printer drones. We could talk about drones, Obama, the hospital
they bombed in Afghanistan, the doctors they killed, the patients.

Or is that 'we' bombed, killed? You'd know. We could talk about Oregon.
God knows, you'd sputter about Trump. We could talk over the steam.
I'd turn the oven on. As it is, I walk the dog, or she walks me. I jiggle lines
of my own. It seems obscene to do these things, to serve the little god
of damage limitation, though you did, too. You got the dosage wrong.

The little god makes no promises. She's like the Oracle at Delphi,
a place that charmed us all, clear cold water falling over rocks
delivering her prophecies so gently, musically, or like the Sibyl
scribbling on leaves that scatter to the four winds, sweeping through
the house, the bones, the meat. She likes the verb *to sweep.*

She knows it contains *weep*. She likes *cook*, with the o's.
Make, next to *ache*. All these verbs-- she's a Via Negativa,
not taken to the end unless she loses you. She has a short
attention span. The little god of damage limitation lives here
in the kitchen, listens to corkscrew and kettle gasp and sob.

Dear Window Again,

You run in my family on the female side
your sand and fire running in place while

giving an impression of stability, until
the hairline fractures show. The rosary

my mother's mother held like an umbilical
sitting at the window looking down over

the Bronx police station, cops going up
and down the steps, wrecks towed to

the curb. She prayed for all their souls,
curbing hers until it got away and drove

her crazy. My mother's broke in waves,
angers that flared and flamed and banked

till next time. She loved windows, though,
watching the birds through the thin pane

hummingbirds like homunculi, red cardinals
against the snow she hated, lighting a fire for her,

the little match girl. I tinker with the word
Defenestration, from the French, fenêtre,

prefer window, made of wind and ow.
I don't do rosaries now, that ghost piano

I used to play, fingers tapping the pillow,
no beads. I listen to the crying doves,

wood pigeons, crane for herons from the train.
When I see one, it's not the same as it was,

but there in the middle of the field, where
the lake has formed in my time here, like he

stood in the middle of my life in the lake he made.
My life is dry. I look and see. I try. The heron flies.

Tapers

Tapers are skinny candles
like fingers, for holding
at vigils, outside prisons,
in the low light of temples -

- you get the picture
You always got the picture.
That was never the issue.

Too many pictures, too
quickly. You needed to taper,
see by a lesser light,

a skinnier candle,
a flicker in the night.
Something you could handle.

Later, doing a taper
off Valium,
under the doctor,

you hated the Valium fog.
Impatient, you found
a quicker antidote than time.

In a safe dose.
In a safe place.

Most accidents happen
in the home.

Your heart, maybe.
An arrhythmia,
the doctor thought.

Maybe. No one knew
or knows or ever will,
only that you don't
show up for anything,

no corkscrew winkles
you out of your room
with a decisive pull,
no smell of bourguignon
smokes you out now,

nothing boots up
your computer
or your brain.
Nothing makes you
angry, shakes
loud laughter
from your frame.

I don't even
dream you
yet. I write these
stupid poems
to stay put.

You'd get that
I'm a taper
in the window,
waiting.

Ibiza

The cheap kitchen radio I found
in Birkenhead is called Ibiza,
a name I re-read every day, soon

won't see. You'd know how much
I need a new kitchen radio. The market
only had a DAB. You'd know what

that means, why they wanted seventy
quid. This one cost fifteen. You'd switch
from Radio Four (sometimes Three) to

Five Live, which I found jumpy.
Ibiza is way down the list of places
I regret for you, not somewhere

you'd ever really want to be.
But sometimes I think I'd like
to pack a small bag and take off

for somewhere not like me at all,
where I could disappear from myself,
distilled in crowds of people, invisible

against a landscape that stayed strange,
wear wispy summer stuff, swim way
too far out, even drown without much fuss,

or go on living in some studio, read
books from little shops that cost too much.
Sans computer, forwarding address,

I'd weigh less than a postage stamp,
wither on my bones like fruit on vines
I'd shake my head at for the waste.

I'd have a radio, of course, sometimes
find Five Live on in the middle of the night.
Someone might say *She went to someplace like Ibiza*

where she passed away. That phrase
might be appropriate, for once,
for what I'd do. Like sound waves.

Gobsmacked

Allergic to good people, itchy at the mission,
unfamiliar lately with the smile mechanism,
– stricken with a sense that all this, too, is
a kind of egotism, I hear my old voice say
to you, back when I worked in prison,

I feel like I'm part of the system. We all are,
you point out impatiently. *Ok, ok, you're right,*
I answer you in hindvoice, as I do these days,
get out in the hall to mingle. *Jesus save me*
from the Ladies Bountiful, I imagine people

praying over free Good Shepherd's pie.
Let me eat in peace. But people seem
to welcome company? A yellow woman
(liver cancer, she tells me), right arm in a sling,
says *When I did this, I lost my room at the 'Y'.*

Three nights away, yer out. Told 'em where
I was, in hospital, they said Fair enough,
you can have it back. They gave it to a woman
in her fifties, never been homeless before.
I said let her keep it, I've been on the street lots.

I know how to do it. Gobsmacked, I take
the half – full plate she pushes away, saying
I can't eat much now. You're silent as I
take it to the steamy kitchen filled with good
people and duck out again, quickly. Someone

points to a guy, says *He started the riot at*
Strangeways. I half-disbelieve, but the TV
on the wall shows him, younger, on the roof.
Gave me thirteen extra years for it, he says.
It was worth it. Nobody has to slop out now.

Gobsmacked, I tell the kitchen, want to add
That shows us about being good, but know
you'd hate that way of summing up. I let
the people draw their own conclusions,
listen to your silence in the busy kitchen.

Be Still

After taking the PassionArtTrail 'Be Still', Manchester, 2016*

The back of Manchester Cathedral is clammy,
the front a bossiness of flags. Flags and tombs
in churches never seem right to me. *Did you say fags
and wombs,* you might stage-whisper. In another mood,

It's history, Mother - but you won't be caught dead here.
Standing on tiptoe peering down a huge clay pot made
of concentric pleats I say your name to plant the echo
as if it might grow back into you. I do it at home

in the wind tunnel that leads to the beach. Echoes
get seeded in a lot of places. If you turn the pot on
its side, it becomes a tunnel. So what. I'm too numb
for this exercise. Why come here to balk? Why come

here at all? *Did I bring on this fucking Catholic lapse*
you might ask, or shrug, *Yeah, you would do that.*
On to St. Ann's, in the path laid out by the booklet,
grateful to be following something. Inside the church,

a filmed bell swinging from an arch of rock against the sea,
ringing. Tolling, you could say. I could tear the clapper out
and heave it into the sea. Older than pots or gods,
rocks. Virginia's pocketfuls. You sigh, giggle furiously.

*Makes me think of Woody Allen plugging his nose
into the electrical socket.* Next stop a library of cups,
scarred, still too whole. When we break things at home,
as we do all the time, we try to think it's you breaking

through. Gormley's hanging man has plenty of ropes,
or misplaced umbilicals. Is that why he dangles?
All his mother's fault, those ropey apron strings?
You roll your eyes, *All about you, you mean?* Stopped

at Gwen John's 'Interior', the clutter of her table
while she boils the kettle (strange phrase you, never
a tea drinker, agree), lets it steep. Good word, steep,
for Gwen John pouring herself into the crockery,

the window light, ersatz cross of window frame,
lustre of brown teapot, mother gone when she
was eight, the right way round, at least. You roll
deep-set dark eyes: *Bet she didn't think so,*

but I can't ventriloquize, suspend disbelief,
on the steep train ride home, only feel syllables
beat. *Be still, Be, still be still be still be, still,*
please be still be still be, please, be, still be

artworks mentioned are by Julian Stair (Quietus Revisited), Adam Buick
(Veneration Bell), Rachel Ho, Antony Gormley (Filter), and Gwen John, (Interior).